T0120769

WE HUMANS OVERWHELM OUR EARTH:
11 OR 2 BILLION BY 2100?

DONALD A. COLLINS

authorHOUSE®

AuthorHouse™
1663 Liberty Drive
Bloomington, IN 47403
www.authorhouse.com
Phone: 833-262-8899

© 2021 Donald A. Collins. All rights reserved.

No part of this book may be reproduced, stored in a retrieval system, or
transmitted by any means without the written permission of the author.

Published by AuthorHouse 06/24/2021

ISBN: 978-1-6655-3015-6 (sc)
ISBN: 978-1-6655-3014-9 (e)

Library of Congress Control Number: 2021913033

Print information available on the last page.

Any people depicted in stock imagery provided by Getty Images are models,
and such images are being used for illustrative purposes only.
Certain stock imagery © Getty Images.

This book is printed on acid-free paper.

Because of the dynamic nature of the Internet, any web addresses or
links contained in this book may have changed since publication and
may no longer be valid. The views expressed in this work are solely those
of the author and do not necessarily reflect the views of the publisher,
and the publisher hereby disclaims any responsibility for them.

DEDICATION

Dedicated to Sarah G. Epstein with whom I've shared a blissful journey for 27 years.

CONTENTS

INTRODUCTION

World Leaders continue to Ignore our Human Population Crisis.

The Sunday, June 6, 2021, 60 Minutes featured to my delight the 95-year-old UK naturalist Sir David Attenborough who told us how in his lifetime (and mine @ 90) human behavior has despoiled our only home, Earth!

Despite my decades-long affection for 60 Minutes, I was extremely disappointed by what had to be their editorial decision not to allow Sir David to make the case for why our planet is being murdered—despite admitting it has been— the growth of human numbers in his lifetime from 2 billion to 8 billion with 3 billion more likely as climate change progresses!

I have quoted Sir David, E.O. Wilson, and other respected scholars often in the pieces you will read here. The fear of not enough human growth that prompted Xi Jinping, China's leader, to authorize women to have 3 children may not happen as women worldwide gain control of their fertility.

How do we keep a habitable planet? Not by destroying nonrenewable resources on a finite planet while our government and others help fund rich men to build rocket toys to take people to our uninhabitable moon or a planet like Mars as we continue to murder our planet and not spend the modest money (<u>$20 billion per year Lester Brown reported in 2009 in his book *Plan B* on page 263</u>) to ensure people have free family planning services.

Donald A. Collins
Washington DC.
June 16, 2021

CHAPTER 1

OVERPOPULATION: LIMITS GET TESTED AND FAIL!

29 May 2021

As what in my recent Op-eds I have dubbed the "Attenborough crisis"—too many human consumers of Earth's limited resources—we get daily examples such as the page one May 27 Wall Street Journal story entitled "A Grand Plan To Vaccinate The World Unravels" which you can read here.

The climate crisis has caused a growing demand that Exxon, Shell and other fossil fuel producers reduce emissions ASAP!

In a recent TV interview, the 95-year-old master scholar of our natural world's limits, Sir David Attenborough, predicted another 3 billion human consumers will be added if current growth rates prevail. We now have 8 billion human consumers, up from 2 billion in his lifetime.

It is obvious that reductions of all over consumption is now required but far from certain to occur!

It now appears that most likely saviors of humans peacefully continuing to live on Earth over the long term will have to be big corporations, the most enlightened of whom will fear the loss of their hegemonies.

Can enough vaccines be provided for all in this world? Not now on a timely enough basis, but as soon as corporations see the clear self interest in so doing, just as fears about dangerous climate resolutions are now hitting Exxon and Shell.

In short, could profits and fear combine to let corporations save sustainable life on Earth? Let's see.

CHAPTER 2

HUMAN IMPACT IGNORED TOO LONG

24 May 2021

The effect of climate change has now been reaffirmed, but unlike earlier warnings will not go unheeded this time because large commercial interests realize its adverse effect on the whole Earth and the sustainability of human life.

Once again, we must thank the reporting of the world's greatest English language paper, The NY Times whose May 23, 2021, article I cite here.

This again ties directly into the urgency of my current op-ed theme, what I am calling the Attenborough crisis, namely the inability of Earth to sustain its present human numbers. As Sir David, now 95, so eloquently tells us in a recent interview, the number of us has increased at least 3 times in his (and my) lifetime from 2 billion to almost 8 and is going, he thinks, to 11 billion.

Again, the NY Times page one May 23rd article offers us a nuanced view of what a declining birth rate will mean for humans. Read it here.

"The 20th century presented a very different challenge. The global population saw its greatest increase in known history, from 1.6 billion in 1900 to 6 billion in 2000, as life spans lengthened, and infant mortality declined. In some countries — representing about a third of the world's people — those growth dynamics are still in play. By the end of the century, Nigeria could surpass China in population; across sub-Saharan Africa, families are still having four or five children.

But nearly everywhere else, the era of high fertility is ending. As women have gained more access to education and contraception, and as the anxieties associated with having children continue to intensify, more parents are delaying pregnancy and fewer babies are being born. Even in countries long associated with rapid growth, such as India and Mexico, birthrates are falling toward, or are already below, the replacement rate of 2.1 children per family.

...

Demographers warn against seeing population decline as simply a cause for alarm. Many women are having fewer children because that's what they want.

Smaller populations could lead to higher wages, more equal societies, lower carbon emissions and a higher quality of life for the smaller numbers of children who are born."

At 90 I must admit I have in my long life enjoyed the benefits of the vast human excessive use of Earth's non-renewable resources. As I prepare to depart this life, I can only hope my children's generation will help make the dramatic actions necessary to avert the certain disasters of doing nothing!

CHAPTER 3

THE PLANET CAN'T COPE WITH OVERPOPULATION.

19 May 2021

The stories of sightings of what my generation—I'm 90–called UFOs has combined with my perception that life on earth is going to undergo vast changes in the near future for better or for worse! Read about a recent story here.

The COVID pandemic and the George Floyd case revealed untenable inequities which we earthlings must fix to survive.

My recent Op-eds argue that scientific evidence now proves our earth can't support, let alone sustain, its present 8 billion human consumers! You can reread my Op-ed about this proven case here.

Credible scientific projections suggest we could add billions more humans, but climate disasters and human conflicts likely will make our survival increasingly less likely unless we reduce human numbers ASAP!

Remember when the 17th Century Catholic Church hierarchy put the Italian astronomer Galileo in jail—actually confined him, in-house-arrested, in his home—for saying our earth rotated around the sun?

Now, our Supreme Court may reduce women's right to choose abortion after 15 weeks, long before quickening—the ability of a fetus to survive outside a mother's womb! Only possible, because Donald Trump packed our Supreme Court with ideologues during his disastrous tenure.

Birth control options abound now, but free distribution and use keeps getting inhibited by religious fantasy that argues limitations on fertility are somehow evil while limitations on war and minor human conflicts are worth retaining.

But most importantly, this situation exists because of the universal failure of leaders to acknowledge the urgency of this oncoming global tragedy, the existing excess of human numbers, which could be addressed now inexpensively, safely, and voluntarily to all who wished it.

Reality better start to follow science instead of buying fantasies like the big lie about who won the November 3rd election as continuing to be believed by 25 percent of American voters, destroying the credibility of the GOP.

But the primary recognition must begin by acknowledging Earth can't sustain its present human numbers. Failure to recognize that verity puts humans on the path to denigration so horrible that COVID will seem like a minor cold.

And how about urgent need to share COVID vaccine cures? Doing so could be a major impetus to convince the world's citizens that unless we realize the overshoot of planetary numbers we are doomed to perpetual wars and conflicts which inhibit reaching a long-term era of tranquility and human progress.

Will the George Floyd conviction initiate the timely death of American racism? Could be! But much more needs to be done.

Speaking of racism, certainly the main racial discrimination done over history so far has been against women and ensuring their full rights, particularly their reproductive right not to bear children if they wish! Progress is happening as daily stories like this appear. Read here.

If such evil biases are not set aside, these conditions assure the disastrous future guaranteed by our ignoring human overshoot!

Maybe then those UFOs will decide to land on earth and salvage what is left.

CHAPTER 4

RECOGNIZING THE POPULATION PROBLEM IS NOW VITAL

18 May 2021

One vital element I neglected to mention in <u>my last Op-ed</u> as fundamental to taking action in reducing world population, is the threat of rampant tribalism!

In no way was I suggesting that any single group be featured to be reduced in number. Instead, governments and private institutions should offer all people free and voluntary means to have the number of children they desire. Unlike the GOP now seeking to make voting harder for minorities, I want to make everyone's decisions about parenting totally voluntary and accessible.

My main point was to make sure that all people understand that the present number of human consumers of our finite planet's limited resources had already exceeded sustainable limits as scientific evidence has made clear.

This then is what calls upon the world's major stronghold of democracy, the USA, to strengthen itself and encourage others to recognize the threat presented by excess human numbers, and to support benign non mandatory actions to offer free family planning services to all who seek them.

Quick calculations can confirm that the cost of providing such options compared to the present cost of military resources is extremely small.

Therefore, recognizing the overwhelming population problem now becomes vital if we are to solve it with the least disruption possible.

And who better to lead such an immense effort than the USA?

The facts as so powerfully presented by Steven Johnson in his May 2nd NY Times Magazine article, and the work of other credible scientists for decades about planetary limits, seem to me to coalesce as the perfect example around the global pandemic now assaulting all humanity. In treating this threat, we learn the interconnected nature of all our human lives! You can reread my last Op-ed and Johnson's article here.

Thus, we now must-see sustainable survival for all creatures and the natural resources that sustain us and globally must recognize the similarity of all tribes as having needs which must be achieved if we humans are to survive in relative peace and prosperity.

CHAPTER 5

OVERPOPULATION NOW NEEDS WORLDWIDE ATTENTION AND ACTION

15 May 2021

The scientific truth from the Attenboroughs of the world is that the Earth cannot sustain habitable life even for its present 8 billion humans and the countless other animals and plants. That humans are overconsuming is now proven beyond doubt.

Such news sadly does not seem to appear on most human radars, but its evidence appears daily in worldwide mass media stories of violence, mayhem, and shortages of all kinds over which humans naturally contend with increasing intensity.

What now? Since 25 percent of GOP voters now seem willing to ignore credible data, so of course they may all be likely to ignore the fact of my above initial paragraph, just as they refuse to wear face masks and still think Trump is great for undermining our democracy with his big lie.

Sadly, more credible, and powerful leaders such as our own President or China's Chi and most others don't fully get Attenborough's message either!

Bottom line: Fixing—is that possible? —the climate crisis alone won't solve the population crisis.

Only making the means of birth control available to everyone can we gradually, voluntarily, and peacefully reduce human numbers to sustainable levels.

Facing the above facts, we know about the long opposition from religion and the addiction of commercial interests to endless growth.

Here's my take on how to talk to both of these previously intransigent constituencies!

By Widely Informing Religionists and Commercial Interests That They Could Be Planetary Saviors!!

For years, those of us who fought for reproductive choice faced constant resistance from religions, particularly for example Roman Catholics about easing abortion restrictions.

Offering women contraceptive choice was also opposed vigorously by many religious people.

Now, as proof of planetary survival and/or wellbeing has been put in serious jeopardy by credible scientific information, would these pushers of their special credos of faith find the morality of saving the whole planet with all its creatures both human, animal, and natural a basis for reevaluation of their governing behavior?

Likewise, faced with irrefutable facts about where human life on planet earth is headed, wouldn't the kind of irresponsible greed and focus on wealth's ability to gain temporal power lose a huge measure of its appeal? In both cases I can hear you say, "Probably not."

Possible Positive Answer: It only would happen in substantial numbers if these constituencies believed this now serious scientifically proven fact of urgent planetary people limitation.

And judging from our inability to "sell" that burgeoning story for decades why am I very optimistic about selling its credibility now?

Because so many people from all over our finite globe have arrived at a new understanding of the unacceptable consequences of doing nothing!

How can the power of Steven Johnson's May 2, 2021 NY Times Magazine article be ignored if widely known and understood by the constituencies above?

We can thank this next add-on from Population Institute of Canada's Bill Rees for his confirming testimony about the urgency for population limitation, again quoting Sir David Attenborough.

It's wakeup time, Folks.

CHAPTER 6

THE DAILY NEWS HEADLINES WE SEE OF GLOBAL VIOLENCE CONFIRMS OUR NEED FOR VOLUNTARY FAMILY PLANNING.

12 May 2021

In watching the daily news, we lucky Americans can mostly find ourselves less estranged from human traumas than most of the rest of the humans on our finite planet.

However, we know from the carefully documented history — see The NY Times Magazine's <u>May 2nd article</u> by David Johnson — that our brilliance in solving smallpox and most other major killer diseases, caused human average lifespans to double from about 45 to much higher in the past hundred years, creating the population explosion from 2 billion in about 1930 to at least 8 billion by 2030.

Reputable scientists ascribe our climate crisis and escalating environmental disasters to that growth, but instead of seeking peaceful, voluntary, less costly ways to encourage fewer births, calls for limitless growth on our finite planet keep coming from the world's most powerful leaders!

So, as I have noted before, the most well-funded birth control programs now in use feature wars, famine, disease, and pestilence when for far less our world leaders could buy all of living humankind voluntary, safe, effective ways to avoid unwanted births and gradually reduce our numbers to sustainable levels.

We know why this totally credible path will likely not be chosen, don't we?

How about rigid religious demands for orthodoxy, relentless human greed, unchecked racism, and the hatred that those human failings generate??

Just watching this process unfold sparked that precocious, brave young Greta Thunberg to raise hopes for benign urgent action from the rich and powerful which seems yet to have gotten little beyond vast media noise!

As Wikipedia tells us

> "Greta Tintin Eleonora Ernman Thunberg is a Swedish environmental activist who is internationally known for challenging world leaders to take immediate action for climate change mitigation. Thunberg initially gained notice for her youth and her straightforward speaking manner, both in public and to political leaders and assemblies, in which she criticizes world leaders for their failure to take what she

considers sufficient action to address the climate crisis.

Thunberg's activism started after persuading her parents to adopt several lifestyle choices to reduce their own carbon footprint. In August 2018, at age 15, she started spending her school days outside the Swedish Parliament to call for stronger action on climate change by holding up a sign reading Skolstrejk för klimatet (School strike for climate). Soon other students engaged in similar protests in their own communities. Together they organised a school climate strike movement under the name Fridays for Future. After Thunberg addressed the 2018 United Nations Climate Change Conference, student strikes took place every week somewhere in the world. In 2019, there were multiple coordinated multi-city protests involving over a million students each. To avoid flying, Thunberg sailed to North America where she attended the 2019 UN Climate Action Summit. Her speech there, in which she exclaimed "how dare you", was widely taken up by the press and incorporated into music.

Her sudden rise to world fame has made her both a leader and a target for critics, especially due to her age. Her influence on the world stage has been described by The Guardian and other newspapers as the "Greta effect". She received numerous honours and awards, including an honorary Fellowship of the Royal Scottish Geographical Society, inclusion in Time's 100 most influential people, being the youngest Time Person of the Year, inclusion in the Forbes list of The World's 100 Most Powerful Women (2019), and three consecutive nominations for the Nobel Peace Prize (2019–2021)."

That Wikipedia quote sounds great, but the substantial action needed is far from happening. If peaceful sustainable human survival is to be achieved those in power better cause urgent action soon.

Populating our moon or colonizing Mars while destroying our precious earthly assets seems madness worthy of reevaluation!

Anybody listening?

Here are a few items from the Washington Post May 11th of just the last 24 hours of mass murders, bombings, etc. the list is overwhelming!!!

Jerusalem clashes widen across Israel; Gaza fighting escalates — <u>The Washington Post</u>

Africa coronavirus variants: Monitoring increases while vaccinations lag — <u>The Washington Post</u>

Deadly 'black fungus' cases add to India's covid crisis — <u>The Washington Post</u>

At least 9 dead in rare Russian school shooting — <u>The Washington Post</u>

And the above is just a fraction of the horror stories the daily media output provides us.

CHAPTER 7

WASHINGTON POST'S POPULATION GROWTH CRISIS STORY IGNORES SURFEIT OF PEOPLE

11 May 2021

Page one on its left column the <u>Washington Post's May 10, 2021,</u> story by Dan Balz its headline screams "A blinking light ahead: Slowing population growth raises questions about America as a land with unlimited horizons" and then laboriously argues that the lack of adding more people is destroying America's future!

That new immigrants are vital elements to keeping our economy renewing itself is not what I am arguing here.

What I am arguing is the global growth of human numbers and the absence of that recognition that we have already exceeded the capacity of our planet to service the present 8 billion here now.

And then the likely addition of at least another billion as the chaos that such numbers are already bringing to our climate and environment and the unlikely future of global peace!

Many of my Op-eds have made this warning which noted that world population has grown in my 90-year lifetime from 2 billion to almost 8 billion, an unsustainable level according to top environmental experts.

The NY Times Magazine's <u>May 2nd issue</u> which featured the writing of Steven Johnson noted that after we learned how to stop most diseases we caused world population to explode. The likely future of more pandemics is assured by most experts.

No mention of these facts in the WP's mindless warning about lack of growth.

Instead of lauding possible population stability and suggesting organizing ways to encourage reduction in human numbers, the mad desire for endless human growth on a planet of finite size seems to encourage our outward push to populate the moon and Mars while we savage the Amazon Rain Forrest and kill off species after species of non-human creatures.

Instead of fostering a benign voluntary global family planning program, we humans engage in endless wars and human conflicts which can kill a lot of people but not solve the human excess problem successfully.

Choice about parenting remains elusively stymied by religious and cultural taboos which, if unchanged, will destroy a peaceful global future.

Proof? Just check the daily news as worldwide turmoil enlarges.

My children and theirs will likely reap the whirlwind of my generation's failure to act to deal with the pandemic of excess human numbers!

CHAPTER 8

BIRTH CONTROL IS THE MOST URGENT ISSUE WE MUST SOLVE.

6 May 2021

<u>The May 2, 2021, issue of the New York Times Magazine</u> is devoted to a careful history of how our huge scientific and managerial skills have changed human longevity so as to create the population explosion now endangering human livability on Earth.

You might even, as I did, read this seminal article out loud to a family member to fully capture its power and complexity as fashioned by its author Steven Johnson so as to leave no doubt as to why birth control becomes the most urgent issue we must solve or destroy ourselves!

Earlier articles posted on this site by such luminaries as E.O. Wilson and Sir David Attenborough have so eloquently made this case, but the Times issue explains so sharply at the end of this long piece the ultimate irony of our triumph over disease as having created a certain path to our own human self-destruction!

Here is the article's author Steven Johnson's take on what our progress in combating disease has produced.

"All those brilliant solutions we engineered to reduce or eliminate threats like smallpox created a new, higher-level threat: ourselves. Many of the key problems we now face as a species are second-order effects of reduced mortality. For understandable reasons, climate change is usually understood as a byproduct of the Industrial Revolution, but had we somehow managed to adopt a lifestyle powered by fossil fuels without reducing mortality rates — in other words, if we had invented steam engines and coal-powered electrical grids and automobiles but kept global population at 1800 levels — climate change would be much less of an issue. There simply wouldn't be enough humans to make a meaningful impact on carbon levels in the atmosphere.

Runaway population growth — and the environmental crisis it has helped produce — should remind us that continued advances in life expectancy are not inevitable. We know from our recent history during the industrial age that scientific and technological progress alone do not guarantee positive trends in human health. Perhaps our increasingly interconnected world — and dependence on industrial livestock, particularly chickens — may lead us into what some have called an age of pandemics, in which Covid-19 is only a preview of even more deadly avian-flu outbreaks. Perhaps some rogue technology — nuclear weapons, bioterror attacks — will kill enough people to reverse the great escape. Or perhaps it will be the environmental impact of 10 billion people living in industrial societies that will send us backward. Extending our lives helped give us the climate crisis. Perhaps the climate crisis will ultimately trigger a reversion to the mean.

No place on earth embodies that complicated reality more poignantly than Bhola Island, Bangladesh. Almost half a century ago, it was the site of one of our proudest moments as a species: the elimination of variola major, realizing the dream that Jenner and Jefferson had almost two centuries before. But in the years that followed smallpox eradication, the island was subjected to a series of devastating floods; almost half a million people have been displaced from the region since Rahima Banu contracted smallpox there. Today large stretches of Bhola Island have been permanently lost to the rising sea waters caused by climate change. The entire island may have disappeared from the map of the world by the time our children and grandchildren celebrate the centennial of smallpox eradication in 2079.

What will their life spans look like then? Will the forces that drove so much positive change over the past century continue to propel the great escape? Will smallpox turn out to be just the first in a long line of threats — polio, malaria, influenza — removed from Jefferson's "catalog of evils"? Will the figurative rising tide of egalitarian public health continue to lift all the boats? Or will those momentous achievements — all that unexpected life — be washed away by an actual tide?"

Clearly the enlightened among us are encouraging implementation of obvious steps to be taken, but facing ourselves as the enemy is the ultimate blind spot.

The safe and benign and surest avenues to the reduction of human numbers is providing complete contraceptive choices to couples who contemplate parenting.

Instead, it would seem the most powerful and extensive birth control methods we are offering are widespread killing through wars generated by greed, ethnic hatred, and racism!

CHAPTER 9

WHEN DO ALL PEOPLE PRIORITIZE FAMILY PLANNING?

3 April 2021

As we observe the effects worldwide of not only the current pandemic, but we daily observe, in our now instantaneous news coverage, the breakdowns of decent life in many countries where such trauma had never occurred before!

Inevitably, the source of the problem has been too many people! Planetary human numbers are now nearly up to 8 billion people worldwide from only 2 when I was born in 1931.

Multiple solutions are put forward, but the subject of excess humans seldom gets on the priority list.

More people equal more customers, more worshipers, more economically indigent workers in the burgeoning age of automation!

Preaching for fewer people has not proved able to keep human numbers from exploding and now we are at a planetary resource meltdown which must be addressed worldwide!

The powerful BBC film coming out this month featuring Sir David Attenborough on overpopulation's effect on our future should finally trigger action, but I doubt it will!

Our downward heading from here could be swift and horrific.

The ultimate family planning program will be, as it has been for so long, provided by war, famine, disease, and death, but the diminution of the resources needed for even a largely diminished number of humans will not be adequate and the danger for more declines in the welfare of those remaining is heightened.

When the factor of global warming is added, one can hardly envision a route to recovery.

Special thanks for this likely outcome can be shared by the world's religions, the fabulous expansion powers of our commercial enterprises and the indifference of all of us to the rise of the scourge of too many people.

So, who are those we consider "too many?"

And that of course is why any sane solution is likely impossible. Our record of racist behavior which we now confront in the USA has echoed before throughout human history.

Attenborough's tentative optimism is laudable and indeed could cause alterations in human behavior which would indeed be remarkable.

I won't be around to learn the outcome, but I recognize I have lived in a relatively safe place in history despite the world's entry in my lifetime into a time when nuclear war is entirely possible, but as yet only been tried once!

Move to Mars? Who else is out there in vastness of space?

The ultimate faith by humans as we see the decline of many religions will be having the will to go on positively by fostering smart, secular, steps like being less racist, less religiously doctrinaire, less violent, and less greedy?

Any takers?

CHAPTER 10

DON'T MISS "8 BILLION ANGELS" A VIMEO TRAILER ON THE CERTAIN HUMAN DESTRUCTION AS OUR EXCESS HUMAN NUMBERS ARE OVERUSING OUR PLANET'S RESOURCES! A SOLUTION NEEDS ALL OF US

1 April 2021

As COVID-19 has graphically demonstrated, we are all of one world—a small planet being made rapidly unfit for many more humans than at present.

Since my birth in 1931, we have added nearly 6 billion people to the planet as our total number now is approaching eight billion.

In April, we are told now by a Vimeo trailer film entitled "8 Billion Angels" that Vimeo will offer a new film about how as rapacious humans, our present numbers are rushing us humans to our own deaths as we kill the very life sustaining assets that keep us alive!!

While we could possibly solve urgent issues such as racism and gun control and a myriad of other problems, if we keep killing our irreplaceable natural resources nothing else will matter.

Dictators won't solve this future collision, but neither can the world's most well-armed democratic government— us!! It will take us all.

Mexican Border crisis? Biden could offer to bear the cost to take any unaccompanied child to his or her native country if their safety could be assured.

Probably not feasible, but neither is our continuing rape of Planet Earth.

A major UN Conference featuring speakers like Sir David Attenborough and Professor E.O. Wilson would get so much big media coverage! TV could show the expressions on the faces of leaders such as Chi, Biden and other world leaders listening to these irrefutable facts. Would they wince or frown or ever verbalize the obvious truth of what is happening? Would the fact that we have already destroyed two thirds of the planet's tropical rain forests make an impression?

Or are we U.S. citizens too preoccupied with basketball's March Madness or the chance marijuana will be legalized to care about such an abstract future reality?

Following such a well-publicized UN meeting, would these powerful leaders do anything? What? Offering free family planning to anyone who wants it? Or would religionists get antsy?

Certainly, the current TV coverage of the George Floyd murder trial should bring a better understanding about American racism's impact to many previously unmoved people. Why not ensuring a better future for all of us by taking action now on overpopulation?

Could a major UN Conference help by boosting support for climate change and understanding about the certain diminution of future human wellbeing due to overpopulation? Maybe not but it is surely worth trying.

CHAPTER 11

NO ORDINARY TIME FOR HUMANS

19 June 2020

Never on this planet has electronic information access been so readily available to so many people, but especially to the world leaders who are in positions to make meaningful decisions for constructive changes based on available data!

In fact, our rapidly and overpoweringly proliferating electronic mass media now puts up data on virtually everything that can be measured. We have hardly any excuse to not see trends and problems faster and more clearly than ever before in our history.

Take for example the ironic example about those daily instant facts about the Coronavirus outbreak which Martin Smith so perfectly told us the history about on Frontline. Unfortunately, as we learn daily that information was not effectively used to save human lives and the prospect for viral resurgence is reported daily in multiple places both here and abroad.

As my readers know, my recent op-ed pieces have emphasized the dangers of the size of human numbers in the world. That number, which in my lifetime (born

1931), has exploded from 2 billion to almost 8 billion with experts projecting that there will be 10 billion of us by the 2050's.

In short, to borrow Doris Kearns Goodwin's 1994 book title *No Ordinary Time*, that we urgently need to recognize that for all of us humans now is no ordinary time.

It took a meteor hit in the Yucatán some 60 million years ago to end the age of the dinosaurs. As the result of marvelous scientific sleuthing, we have tracked Earth's origins from its start 4.5 billion years ago to now. From the then fiery hurtling massive rocks to the cooling surfaces without oxygen, to our presently habitable Earth, the evolution was amazing just as was our ability to deduce that prior history from examinations of the physical evidence in rocks and fossils. Those collections of dinosaur bones were just a first step in the progress we have made in analyzing our planetary history.

Now however, staring us in the face is the concept of limits! I challenge you to find someone reporting what those ultimate limits for human numbers might be.

ABC Science environment reporter Nick Kilvert for Life Matters, told us in 2019,

> "If Australians want to continue living as we do without making any changes, and as a planet we want to meet our footprint, then the number of humans Earth can sustain long term is around 1.9 billion

people, which was roughly the global population 100 years ago in 1919."

We can surmise that with the present human conflicts around our world, environmental destruction, and general poverty there will be much human despair. If we value and see democracy and human freedom as exemplary goals for humans, such conditions will likely not survive as human numbers continue to expand at 76 million or so annually.

So, as we watch the current U.S. presidential campaign rattle on sadly with neither party at all engaged in pondering this most critical question about the future wellbeing of humans, we are unlikely to hear either candidate, or for that matter, any other powerful world leader taking up the cudgel for the only benign solution to this pending human disaster.

That solution has been posed by experts for decades but blocked in its path by powerful traditional enemies of equity and freedom.

As David Attenborough states so clearly, women must be given full access to reproductive freedom and equal political rights which have long been widely denied to women worldwide. As Attenborough notes if women had these freedoms, it has been widely demonstrated already that women will have fewer children if so empowered.

That's the benign solution. The other avenues to no solution are vicious, undemocratic, and dangerous. Also well proven daily now by stories in the mass media.

Biden's choice for a woman Vice Presidential running mate is good, just as Obama's selection and service as a two term President was widely viewed by a substantial majority of American voters as a vitally progressive occurrence.

But the time is very late and the urgency of activating broad effective actions for women's freedom is certainly not felt by enough world leaders.

Both secular and religious enemies for change have inhibited the necessary power shift to women's rights although U.S. women have increasingly gained some of those rights in this century.

It is indeed no ordinary time, and the meteor of destruction that killed the dinosaurs will not likely strike our planet now with the numerous alert systems in place to guard against such a possibility.

Yes, Coronavirus is a major factor now unsolved, as is our frightening ignorance about racism which is a worldwide condition. But the pressures of human numbers will prove to be the dominant force in creating conditions which will make our lives increasingly unstable and unsustainable!

The true irony is that this really major threat to human life was best stated by that famous cartoon character Pogo

Possum, a <u>daily comic strip</u> that was created by cartoonist <u>Walt Kelly</u> and was syndicated to American newspapers from 1948 until 1975. It has since been revived.

Wikipedia <u>describes</u> Pogo as "An amiable, humble, philosophical, personable, everyman opossum. Kelly described Pogo as 'the reasonable, patient, softhearted, naive, friendly person we all think we are' in a 1969 TV Guide interview. The wisest (and probably sanest) resident of the swamp, he is one of the few major characters with sense enough to avoid trouble. Though he prefers to spend his time fishing or picnicking, his kind nature often gets him reluctantly entangled in his neighbors' escapades. He is often the unwitting target of matchmaking by Miz Beaver (to the coquettish Ma'm'selle Hepzibah), and has repeatedly been forced by the swamp's residents to run for president, always against his will. He wears a simple red and black striped shirt and (sometimes) a crushed yellow fishing hat. His kitchen is well known around the swamp for being fully stocked, and many characters impose upon him for meals, taking advantage of his generous nature. His full name is Ponce de Leon Montgomery County Alabama Georgia Beauregard Possum—a parody of the blueblood aristocracy of the Old South!"

As you recall, Pogo's most famous pronouncement was "We have met the enemy and he is us!" There's a lot of wisdom in Kelly's strip!

CHAPTER 12

HUMAN NUMBERS ARE AFFECTING EVERYTHING INCLUDING WORLD PEACE AND SURVIVAL

17 June 2020

That seems to be the rule these days. Never mention human numbers as a factor in loss of democracy, decent livelihood, environmental protections, etc.

However, IPS News did another article on June 12th about global poverty moving to Middle Income developing nations in Asia, with a photo and caption focus on India.

The IPS piece begins by saying, "Global poverty, which is increasing because of the economic impact of the coronavirus crisis and ensuing worldwide lockdowns, is shifting and a dramatic increase in middle-income developing countries in Asia is expected."

"This is according to new research published by the United Nations University World Institute for Development Economics Research (UNU-WIDER)."

IPS News has not failed as so many have to mention the population impact, with this paragraph which appears as an insert on its first page.

"As the world's population grows at a pace of some 76 million people per year, so do the challenges associated with it. Increased longevity in some regions, juxtaposed with the HIV/AIDS pandemic in others, refugee movements and economic migration all contribute to a changing world demographic in ways that require unique social and policy responses. In the Least Developed Countries (LDCs), the population is expected to triple by 2050, while the ever-increasing demand on the earth's finite natural resources makes it difficult for many to live even at subsistence levels. In this context, family planning and the promotion of sexual and reproductive health have never been more important to empowering women to lead the healthy and productive lives they desire and rendering local and regional population strategies effective."

Of course, the Coronavirus is a factor as the article notes:

"Andy Sumner, a professor of International Development at King's College London and co-author of the report, told IPS that recent research which estimates the number of people who will be pushed into poverty because of the virus also shows that the increase in poverty could be an "absolute increase" for the first time in two decades.

"The potential increase in extreme poverty could mark the first absolute increase in the global count since 1999— and the first since 1990 in terms of the headcount ratio," he told IPS.

The research estimates that the COVID-19 pandemic could push between 80 to 395 million people into extreme poverty globally, under the World Bank's definition of poverty of people living under $1.90 per day. When measured with the World Bank's upper threshold of the poverty line (people living under $3.20 and $5.50 per day) the estimate of people to be pushed into poverty is even higher at more than 500 million people.

Sumner, along with authors Eduardo Ortiz-Juarez of King's College London and Chris Hoy of Australian National University, published the paper titled "Precarity and the pandemic COVID-19 and poverty incidence, intensity, and severity in developing countries" as a follow-up to their April report."

Thus, we come squarely into the main point. Until women get reproductive rights which means the ability to have the number of children they wish, the population situation so succinctly described in the above IPS indented paragraph, the situation will only get worse.

The constant ominous rumblings of pending or on-going wars and increasing civil strife can only accelerate as we learn daily from the media.

In short, we are racing toward disaster, and our leaders are more worried about their re-elections and retention of their personal perks of power! Like Emperor Nero fiddling while Rome burned.

CHAPTER 13

ARE WE HUMANS AN "INVASIVE SPECIES"?

9 May 2020

Humans are the most successful invasive species on the planet, but Earth's resources are not limitless. The National Wildlife Federation tells us that in nature an "'Invasive species'—they may not sound very threatening, but these invaders, large and small, have devastating effects on wildlife."

The article continues, saying,

> "Invasive species are among the leading threats to native wildlife. Approximately 42 percent of threatened or <u>endangered species</u> are at risk due to invasive species.

> "Human health and economies are also at risk from invasive species. The impacts of invasive species on our natural ecosystems and economy cost billions of dollars each year. Many of our commercial, agricultural, and recreational activities depend on healthy native ecosystems."

The NWF article then asks a key question: **What Makes a Species "Invasive"?** It says:

> "An invasive species can be any kind of living organism—an amphibian (like the cane toad), plant, insect, fish, fungus, bacteria, or even an organism's seeds or eggs—that is not native to an ecosystem and causes harm. They can harm the environment, the economy, or even human health. Species that grow and reproduce quickly, and spread aggressively, with potential to cause harm, are given the label "invasive."

> "An invasive species does not have to come from another country. For example, lake trout are native to the Great Lakes, but are considered to be an invasive species in Yellowstone Lake in Wyoming because they compete with native cutthroat trout for habitat."

Read the whole piece here.

So now to us:

What percentage of us in the richest country in the world are living paycheck to paycheck? Many! Are we invasive consumers? Do we think at all about our use or misuse of planetary resources? Are we aware that in my 89 years of life our human numbers have gone from 2 billion to almost 8 billion?

Jim Kramer, my favorite stock market voice who hosts Mad Money beginning at 6 pm Eastern time on CNBC, was interviewing the CEO of a company that makes ersatz meat, called Beyond Meat.

Meat shortages are increasing and likely to continue even when the meat producers recent shut down comes back.

Jim's question to the ersatz meat guy was roughly as I recall, "Can your firm ramp up to meet the increased demand?" After which Jim noted in an almost sidebar comment that the planet will have 10 billion people by 2050. As if that meant nothing but more good growth.

We know the world's aquafers are being rapidly depleted and desertification is a common phenomenon around the world but still the call for more growth is unceasing!

On TV one morning recently, the announcer bemoaned the fact that big African Game Park tourism was down but now it has been replaced by virtual game tours where guides go out and film what they find and simulcast it for paying at home clients.

The media daily shows us scenes of the growing anger of unserved millions of people, but achievable fixes for their plight are not offered even though we know that more violence and civil disruption is spreading rapidly.

That the UN, as I have suggested in an earlier piece, might convene a major world powers meeting. Purpose: To frankly discuss these burgeoning troubles which have not been mentioned by any major leader amid the daily reports of sniping back and forth between the U.S. and China and nasty personal attacks on public figures.

Limits to growth are exhibited everywhere, as at least half the world's nearly 8 billion humans vie for the necessities of life. And endless growth on our finite planet remains the priority mantra of businesses everywhere.

Are we humans "an invasive species"? Isn't the answer obvious to anyone who thinks about it? Are our leaders too frightened to be honest about telling us the facts?

Oh, by the way, originality is not what I am claiming here. Another piece with almost this same title was published in the NY Times on December 6, 2017. You can read it here.

CHAPTER 14

TOO MANY EXPERTS FAIL TO NOTE POPULATION AS OUR ROOT PROBLEM

14 April 2020

My recent op ed "Is The Urgent World Population Limitation Message Finally To Be Heeded At Last?" expressed the long held opinion of many of my colleagues that the world had become overpopulated and that this virus was yet another symptom of that long developing fact.

Yet the commentaries from the many distinguished gurus I've read recently fail to mention excess world population as the primary de facto exploiter of our fragile planet's limited resources.

Find a vaccine and go on our merry way seems to be the attitude of most, ignoring the burgeoning examples of our greedy and destructive planetary behavior.

Reading the views of Yale historian Frank Snowden recently I eagerly looked for his backing on the effect of population growth.

He makes passing mentions to population. Here were all I found.

> "Today, in the industrial world, it would be unthinkable that cholera could ravage the city of New York or Paris or Rome because we have robust sanitary infrastructures. In resource-poor settings it is different, because they have the kinds of conditions that I was talking about.
>
> On the other hand, we are nearly 8 billion people, and we live in enormous cities that are hugely congested, and all of those cities are linked by rapid air travel, so what happens medically in Jakarta in the morning can happen in New Haven and Paris by the evening. With all these international linkages created by globalization, there is an opportunity for a very different kind of disease to flourish, and it seems that coronavirus is now exploiting this very condition.

How has our relationship with the environment helped to spur epidemics?

The world we've created is so populous, and also so unregulated and greedy that we have enormously invaded the habitat of wild animals. That is putting extraordinary pressure on them, so human beings are forcibly brought into contact with species that may be reservoirs of an extraordinary range of diseases that human populations have never encountered before.

We can see this in Ebola, where the palm industry invaded the forests of West Africa, felled the trees, and drove out the bats. There are many, many hundreds of species of bats, and many of those species harbor hundreds of coronaviruses. Many of them are lethal to human beings."

He delineates cause but doesn't close the logical loop— that too many people remain at the heart of sustained human well-being!

He is certainly not alone in failing to mention the root cause of where we are going, human expansion.

I so often take pride in the fact that I was lucky enough with such modest academic credentials from my high school to gain a place in the 1949 freshman class at Yale which in those days of small depression era cohorts virtually guaranteed employment upon graduating.

Equally amazed at graduating, I and my Korean War era grads were faced with being drafted for the Korean War. I lucked out by going to OCS at Newport and 3 plus years as a U.S. Navy officer trolling the Atlantic and

Mediterranean on 2 old Fletcher class destroyers gave me a leadership grad course with pay.

Such credentials upon my Navy exit in 1957 got me a job as a trainee in a large NYC commercial bank where I got, through the GI bill, an MBA at night from NYU.

After returning to my home area in 1962 I helped manage a small venture capital company until in 1965 one of my directors offered me a complete change of career to become an officer managing charitable grant making.

One of this granting group's major priorities was expanding women's reproductive rights.

Since then, I have had the enlightening experience of meeting many top leaders in that family planning arena and discovering how controversial and unfulfilled the obvious virtue of offering women equal rights remains here and elsewhere.

Ironically, those most calling for understanding human frailties are the leaders of religions who are frequently family planning's most bitter enemies.

Lack of access to birth control choice and improved disease controls have zoomed up human numbers since my birth in 1931 from 2 billion worldwide to nearly 8 billion today.

Yes, finding a vaccine deserves priority but failure to limit human numbers will continue to create what will be unsolvable problems. Mother Nature with her virus has sent us a strong message, but we could humanely lower our numbers if we but got her message.

As Dr. Snowden notes, we share this orb with many fauna and flora whose wellbeing sustains us humans!

Will our leaders ever get that main point? It is already very late in being acknowledged, just like our lateness in dealing with COVID-19!

CHAPTER 15

COVID-19 MEANS A WORLDWIDE LESSENING OF RELIGIOUS FANTASY

23 March 2020

As we fight a worldwide epidemic and recognize we as humans "are all in this together" I wanted to take this propitious moment to consider what a potentially massive, huge change in religious viewpoints this Coronavirus crisis may have engendered!

For so much of history humanity has suffered under the yoke of religious beliefs which systematically continue to drive dire discord worldwide.

It is naive for me or anyone to expect such centers of temporal power as the Vatican or Mecca to cede sway over their absurd beliefs, but (and this is the heart of my discourse) anyone who realizes the absurdity of religious fantasy does not have to write an op ed like this or rant against it in the public square! Or suffer great personal danger in so acting.

So how does their power get undermined? Well, it already is very much so lessened in the minds of a huge number of humans worldwide.

I suspect a substantial similar number of people around the world are simply anxious to ignore in their daily lives any deference to insidiously influential beliefs! Proper human conduct is not owned by the Christian 10 commandments, but by the observance of such parts of that list as "thou shall not kill" and not by thou shall put only one god before you!!!

As our solar observations reveal endless other likely habitable worlds out there, the adherence to any fixed orthodoxy becomes more and more absurd.

So why will religion get ultimately back benched!

My opinion: because of the current worldwide efforts to contain and treat Coronavirus.

What a profound message never before posed as it is now with "all hands-on deck" around the world.

Yes, the 1918 Spanish flu infected 300 million people— one quarter of the world's population — and killed 50 to 100 million, but its viral origins were not then discovered. No doubt, grieving those immense human losses was used by religions worldwide to honor the dead. No problem except no cure either.

Humans with science, not some high priest, are heroes and better concrete solvers of this humanistic medical crisis.

Never again will this electronically connected world population be unexposed to this revelation!!

Religious fantasy can no longer be offered as a route to human survival. We humans are in charge and responsible.

What a profound moment which may not be immediately recognized but in a short time (in cosmic terms) organized power-seeking religions will lose face if not place!

There must be some better educational use for St. Patrick's Cathedral and all those other lush palaces of religious righteousness which in time, no doubt, will be found.

Thus, those long time no no's such as access to contraception or safe abortion or the right to die on one's own schedule will be more and more ignored and made accessible by and to the growing numbers of humanistic people who see the light on why freedom from thoughtless religious orthodoxy is vital.

So, whether Pope or others get it, the die is cast and the example of worldwide response to COVID-19 could well in retrospect be seen as the main instigator of relieving humans from religious bondage.

CHAPTER 16

WHY DO NATIONS IDIOTICALLY ADD PEOPLE WHEN BIRTH CONTROL IS CHEAPER THAN GROWTH FOR GROWTH'S SAKE?

28 February 2019

Another urgent admonition from population specialist, Dr. Madeline Weld, Ph.D., President, Population Institute, Canada. Dr. Weld has for years pointed out the failure to address explosive population growth.

Her work deserves support as her message is so clear and unfortunately not replicated often enough by others in a climate where a rising tide of anti-choice voices makes the need for more birth control options versus restrictive religious attacks on choice based on non-secular fantasies.

Her current article cites the new report from the African Development Bank that predicts the need in Africa to "create about 12 million new jobs every year to prevent unemployment from rising."

"Africa: Burgeoning Youth Population, Not Enough Jobs

By Madeline Weld | 28 February 2019

Population Institute Canada

Africa's working-age population could rise from 705 million in 2018 to nearly 1 billion in just over a decade, leading to high unemployment as millions of young people join the labor market and the pressure to provide decent jobs intensifies.

The African Development Bank (AfDB) predicts that at the current rate of labour force growth, Africa would need to create about 12 million new jobs every year to prevent unemployment from rising.

The AfDB's 2019 report concludes that only half of new labour force workers will find employment if current trends continue, which would mean that close to 100 million people could be out of jobs, and that most of the jobs available will be in the "informal sector" – jobs that are neither taxed nor monitored by government.

Coupled with the prospect of high unemployment is the potential for widespread food shortages across the continent. Small-scale farmers constitute 70 percent of people engaged in the agricultural sector in Africa. Many find themselves unable to effectively curb disease and pest outbreaks and, as farm sizes decrease due to the high population growth rate, so too does their food production. The result is that small-scale farmers are earning smaller and smaller incomes, and 65 percent of their households are trapped in a cycle of poverty, surviving on less than $2 a day.

Although agricultural stimulation policies and programs currently aim to increase food production, these efforts are undermined by a high population growth rate, which results in land fragmentation as family farms are divided among offspring, decreasing the chances of large families being able to sustain themselves. And while agricultural production in Africa is starting to feel the effects of climate change, a recent study found that projected rapid population growth will be *the leading cause* of food insecurity and widespread undernourishment across Africa. When the study examined future scenarios with and without the effects of climate change, very little to no difference in undernourishment projections were found, suggesting that population growth is the dominant driver of change.

Even if fertility rates fall substantially in the near future, the youthful age structure of the African population makes it likely that population growth will continue for some time. Given the ominous prospects for employment and food security on the African continent, its leaders should take measures to slow and reverse population growth through education and support for family planning, and governments of developed countries should make those objectives a significant and meaningful part or their foreign aid."

Her work is most deserving of your support.

Weld again cited the imbecility of adding more populations when they can't be employed or fed or properly offered the basic needs of a decent life. We can only expect the results she predicts as creating more and more the kind of upheavals which make daily headlines around the world.

What is the answer to the question I pose in the title of this OP ED? Indifference of elected leaders, religiously ideological opposition to birth control, and most importantly the lack of broad public understanding that such growth will increasingly affect our capacity to survive as a species.

Yes, the onset of global warming, rising terrorism, an inevitable growing malfunctioning of the world's democracies that could ironically lead to even more harsh dictatorships which never end happily.

To the folks who agree the world's fertility is declining, Weld offers a rebuttal which <u>you can read here</u>.

CHAPTER 17

OVERPOPULATION LOOMING PLANETARY DISASTER OUTRANKS ALL OTHER ISSUES

13 August 2018

Readers of my work may recall a previous OP ED in June, in which I repeated my concern about overpopulation as the root cause of disasters now pending as closer to apocalypse for our planet than ever before.

You can refresh your memories here.

CFPUP has so effectively chronicled the adverse effects of powerful monotheistic religions' influence have had on what should be secular matters, perhaps most critically on issues of reproductive choice which has curtailed adequate progress in curbing population growth. Going from about 2 billion people on the planet in 1931, we now have nearly 8 billion humans on our plundered planet, many living under conditions of great distress.

Doubtless, we are all watching the fires in California and the flooding from historic rainfalls here and around the planet as urgent harbingers of dangerous climate change, despite claims of "fake news" emanating from our President and the doxies who follow his increased rantings.

Perhaps if Trump had time away from his tweeting, he could listen to the <u>TED talk of James Hansen</u> whose qualifications on the subject date back to 1990 when his famous paper was presented to Congress with huge recognition there as to its validity.

Reading the Wall Street Journal as I do almost daily, I often find so much to appreciate about its detailed concerns about many issues.

However, just as the commentators on the left, the mention of the primary driver of our growing global pain, population growth, gets virtually no mention. After all there is so much other vital news to consume such as the Paul Manafort trial and whether or not Mr. Trump colluded with the Russians. I say that with no tongue in cheek, just amazement that our planetary house is on fire and under increasing weather distress. We can all see the parallels in the out-of-control wildfires in California and the flooding from historic rains and weather abnormalities.

Could it be that the extreme political dissension in our country which now seems irreconcilable will be healed by a rally to the common defense of our planet?

That would surely mean a swift decline in the fortunes of Mr. Trump.

Lest the left get too excited, getting a cohesively recognizable positive program for change, besides being anti Trump, and for endless government largess along with fully open borders, will not lead to a healing between these extremes.

That the "on the right editorially" Economist Magazine should offer in its <u>August 2nd lead story</u> a boost to action on climate is heartening if not already too late.

Then at virtually the same time, the NY Times Magazine devoted almost its fully August 5, 2018 issue to an even more disturbing article which <u>you can access here</u>.

The article's "Prologue" gives you the point, but the photos give you the tragic fact of our indifference.

> "The world has warmed more than one degree Celsius since the Industrial Revolution. The Paris climate agreement — the nonbinding, unenforceable and already unheeded treaty signed on Earth Day in 2016 — hoped to restrict warming to two degrees. The odds of succeeding, according to a recent study based on current emissions trends, are one in 20. If by some miracle we are able to limit warming to two degrees, we will only have to negotiate the extinction of the world's tropical reefs, sea-level rise of several meters and the abandonment of the Persian Gulf. The climate scientist

James Hansen has called two-degree warming "a prescription for long-term disaster." Long-term disaster is now the best-case scenario. Three-degree warming is a prescription for short-term disaster: forests in the Arctic and the loss of most coastal cities. Robert Watson, a former director of the United Nations Intergovernmental Panel on Climate Change, has argued that three-degree warming is the realistic minimum. Four degrees: Europe in permanent drought; vast areas of China, India and Bangladesh claimed by desert; Polynesia swallowed by the sea; the Colorado River thinned to a trickle; the American Southwest largely uninhabitable. The prospect of a five-degree warming has prompted some of the world's leading climate scientists to warn of the end of human civilization.

Is it a comfort or a curse, the knowledge that we could have avoided all this?

Because in the decade that ran from 1979 to 1989, we had an excellent opportunity to solve the climate crisis. The world's major powers came within several signatures of endorsing a binding, global framework to reduce carbon emissions — far closer than we've come since. During those years, the conditions for success could not have been more favorable. The obstacles we blame for our current inaction had yet to emerge. Almost nothing stood in our way — nothing except ourselves.

Nearly everything we understand about global warming was understood in 1979. By that year, data collected since 1957 confirmed what had been known since before the turn of the 20th century: Human beings have altered Earth's atmosphere through the indiscriminate burning of fossil fuels. The main scientific questions were settled beyond debate, and as the 1980s began, attention turned from diagnosis of the problem to refinement of the predicted consequences. Compared with string theory and genetic engineering, the "greenhouse effect" — a metaphor dating to the early 1900s — was ancient history, described in any Introduction to Biology textbook. Nor was the basic science especially complicated. It could be reduced to a simple axiom: The more carbon dioxide in the atmosphere, the warmer the planet. And every year, by burning coal, oil and gas, humankind belched increasingly obscene quantities of carbon dioxide into the atmosphere.

Why didn't we act? A common boogeyman today is the fossil-fuel industry, which in recent decades has committed to playing the role of villain with comic-book bravado. An entire subfield of climate literature has chronicled the machinations of industry lobbyists, the corruption of scientists and the propaganda campaigns that even now continue to debase the political debate, long after the largest oil-and-gas companies have abandoned the dumb show of denialism. But the coordinated efforts to bewilder the public did not begin in earnest until the end of 1989. During the preceding decade, some of the largest oil companies, including Exxon and Shell, made good-faith efforts to understand the scope of the crisis and grapple with possible solutions.

Nor can the Republican Party be blamed. Today, only 42 percent of Republicans know that "most scientists believe global warming is occurring," and that percentage is falling. But during the 1980s, many prominent Republicans joined Democrats in judging the climate problem to be a rare political winner: nonpartisan and of the highest possible stakes. Among those who called for urgent, immediate and far-reaching climate policy were Senators

John Chafee, Robert Stafford and David Durenberger; the E.P.A. administrator, William K. Reilly; and, during his campaign for president, George H.W. Bush. As Malcolm Forbes Baldwin, the acting chairman of the president's Council for Environmental Quality, told industry executives in 1981, "There can be no more important or conservative concern than the protection of the globe itself." The issue was unimpeachable, like support for veterans or small business. Except the climate had an even broader constituency, composed of every human being on Earth.

It was understood that action would have to come immediately. At the start of the 1980s, scientists within the federal government predicted that conclusive evidence of warming would appear on the global temperature record by the end of the decade, at which point it would be too late to avoid disaster. More than 30 percent of the human population lacked access to electricity. Billions of people would not need to attain the "American way of life" in order to drastically increase global carbon emissions; a light bulb in every village would do it. A report prepared at the request of the White House by the

National Academy of Sciences advised that "the carbon-dioxide issue should appear on the international agenda in a context that will maximize cooperation and consensus-building and minimize political manipulation, controversy and division." If the world had adopted the proposal widely endorsed at the end of the '80s — a freezing of carbon emissions, with a reduction of 20 percent by 2005 — warming could have been held to less than 1.5 degrees.

A broad international consensus had settled on a solution: a global treaty to curb carbon emissions. The idea began to coalesce as early as February 1979, at the first World Climate Conference in Geneva, when scientists from 50 nations agreed unanimously that it was "urgently necessary" to act. Four months later, at the Group of 7 meeting in Tokyo, the leaders of the world's seven wealthiest nations signed a statement resolving to reduce carbon emissions. Ten years later, the first major diplomatic meeting to approve the framework for a binding treaty was called in the Netherlands. Delegates from more than 60 nations attended, with the goal of establishing a global summit meeting to be held about a year later. Among scientists and world leaders, the sentiment was unanimous: Action had to be taken, and the United States would need to lead. It didn't.

The inaugural chapter of the climate-change saga is over. In that chapter — call it Apprehension — we identified the threat and its consequences. We spoke, with increasing urgency and self-delusion, of the prospect of triumphing against long odds. But we did not seriously consider the prospect of failure. We understood what failure would mean for global temperatures, coastlines, agricultural yield, immigration patterns, the world economy. But we have not allowed ourselves to comprehend what failure might mean for us. How will it change the way we see ourselves, how we remember the past, how we imagine the future? Why did we do this to ourselves? These questions will be the subject of climate change's second chapter — call it The Reckoning. There can be no understanding of our current and future predicament without understanding why we failed to solve this problem when we had the chance.

That we came so close, as a civilization, to breaking our suicide pact with fossil fuels can be credited to the efforts of a handful of people, among them a hyperkinetic lobbyist and a guileless atmospheric physicist who, at great personal cost, tried to warn humanity of what was coming. They risked their careers in a painful, escalating campaign to solve the problem, first in scientific reports, later through conventional avenues of political persuasion and finally with a strategy of public shaming. Their efforts were shrewd, passionate, robust. And they failed. What follows is their story, and ours."

Nothing left to say.

Perhaps except this <u>November 19, 2012 from the Big Apple website</u>: "Other than that, Mrs. Lincoln, how did you like the play?"

"Abraham Lincoln (1809–1865) was assassinated in Ford's Theatre on April 14, 1865, while watching the play Our American Cousin. Fletcher Knebel (1911–1993), author of the satirical column about government called "Potomac Fever," wrote in 1957:

"What TV interviewing would have been at the time of the Civil war: 'Well, aside from that, Mrs. Lincoln, what did you think of the play?'"

The classic example of the "sick joke" became popular in 1957 and is still told."

We have a sick planet and seem unable to rouse ourselves from our pursuit of worse tragedy.

CHAPTER 18

WHAT FOOLS WE MORTALS BE, AS WE ALLOW MONOTHEISTIC MALE DOMINATED RELIGIONS TO CONTROL OUR DESTINY

18 January 2015

America had a long-standing missionary tradition which prevailed in large amounts well into the 20th Century. You know, many well intentioned folks set off abroad, going to the heathens in "developing" countries and bringing, as the put down phase noted, "the heathens to the light"—meaning of course to Jesus Christ.

These faithful emissaries also brought useful things like better medical care and often a genuine wish to improve the perceived poor living conditions of their intended targets.

Then of course there were horrific situations of rapacious invasions by foreign powers not for uplifting but for sheer exploitation as in King Leopold's Belgian Congo, which Joseph Conrad immortalized in his classic novelette, *"Heart of Darkness"*.

Now with the astonishing enlightenment of space exploration, we can see our universe as never before. Astronomers have observed the comings and goings of celestial bodies so that they can gainsay that the life of our solar system will surely be limited as in the myriad of other cases they have seen. One estimate is that our system only has another 5 billion years before its "demise". That end of course will simply be to transfer the existing matter here somewhere into another space where for more billions of years it will circulate.

Seems like that puts a new view on all religious beliefs now extant on our planet.

Seems like that gives humans a chance to refigure how we want to spend that time.

Seems like with the present level of religious induced conflict the chance of that is nearly zero.

And yet here we are connected on this tiny planet by our electronic revolution better than ever. We could in the biblical sense reconstitute the Tower of Babel. From the Bible (you pick the version as there are many—see Newsweek January 2-9, 2015):

"Genesis 11:1-9

New International Version (NIV)

The Tower of Babel

Now the whole world had one language and a common speech. As people moved eastward, they found a plain in Shinar and settled there.

They said to each other, "Come, let's make bricks and bake them thoroughly." They used brick instead of stone, and tar for mortar. Then they said, "Come, let us build ourselves a city, with a tower that reaches to the heavens, so that we may make a name for ourselves; otherwise, we will be scattered over the face of the whole earth.""

But the Lord came down to see the city and the tower the people were building. The Lord said, "If as one people speaking the same language, they have begun to do this, then nothing they plan to do will be impossible for them. Come, let us go down and confuse their language so they will not understand each other."

So, the Lord scattered them from there over all the earth, and they stopped building the city. That is why it was called Babel—because there the Lord confused the language of the whole world. From

there the Lord scattered them over the
face of the whole earth."

This story biblical scholars tell us is a parable about too
much human pride. Which brings me (at long last, you
say!) to the point of my piece.

The main conceit of humanity has been and remains the
belief that any particular religious belief is the only one.
Yes, we are fingering the monotheistic male dominated
religions of the world.

My humble computer gets about 100 messages daily from
the ether of all kinds, but among them are always messages
from groups such as LifeNews.com Pro-Life News
Report, offering "Top Stories", such as the headlines
from its 6/2/14 email.

"Current Headlines

Top Stories

- Shocking Government Study Put Lives of
  Premature Babies at Risk
- Their Daughter Only Lived 118 Days, But She
  Brought Them Closer to Eternity
- Obama Admin Willing to Hand Over Terrorists
  but Has No Time for Meriam Ibrahim
- Pro-Abortion Vandal Hangs "Aborted Baby Jesus
  Dolls" Throughout Hobby Lobby Store

More Pro-Life News

- Ryan's Mom Was Raped at 12, But He's Glad He Wasn't Killed in an Abortion
- Nurse Fired for Refusing to Participate in Abortions Files Lawsuit Against the Government
- Ancient Egyptian Mummy of Unborn Baby Shows a Respect for Life, My How Far We've Come
- This Young Mother's Story Imagining Life If She Had Chosen Abortion Will Move You to Tears
- Does Your Local Hospital Do Abortions? It's Time to Find Out and Take Action
- Men and Abortion: The Taboo Topic That Deserves More Attention
- Newborn Kidnapped from Hospital Saved by Four Teens Thanks to Facebook
- Pro-Lifers Shocked That Britain Allows Midwives to Do Abortions
- Court Lets Planned Parenthood Put Women's Lives at Risk with Dangerous Abortion Drug
- British Govt Claims Creating Human Embryos with Three Parents is Perfectly Safe
- Quebec Bill Requires Doctors to Kill Patients Via Euthanasia or Refer to One Who Will
- New Jersey Legislature to Hold Hearing on Bill to Legalize Assisted Suicide
- Former HBO Director Making Pro-Abortion Film Hailing Courageous "Abortion Doctors"

Out of their own mouths the above list of news from these religious sources makes my case. These missionaries for increased human suffering would seek to impose on our secular governance their extreme religious positions. And many times, they have succeeded.

Not to single out just one of these religious monsters, as there are many who know they are communicating directly with God, whoever he or she may be, this tidal wave of violence rises, obviously abetted by the rise of human numbers from 2 billion in 1930 to well over 7 billion now with the prospect of 10 or more billion by the end of this century, which likely will precipitate planetary disruptions previously unseen.

We need but to throw in the urgently real prospect of global warming, precipitated by our unsustainable use of fossil fuels and we seem caught in a vicious circle which seems to offer little hope for resolution sans massive human offings.

The urgency for secular sanity that points to governments not impacted by religious dominance has never been so great.

CHAPTER 19

KEEPING CHURCH SEPARATED FROM SECULAR GOVERNANCE CHARTS A NEAR IMPOSSIBLE ROAD

26 September 2013

Senator Chuck Grassley (R–Iowa): "The constitution does not require the government to exempt churches from federal income taxation or from filing tax and information returns." (Source: The Economist)

As a long-time believer in Mr. Darwin and in only the continuing existence of some of my molecules, not anything even vaguely resembling my present body and mind, I recently visited my beloved, but far away, sister and her marvelous husband, who, as active members of an Anglican church, persuaded me to attend services with them this past Sunday.

Despite my once parent guided membership in a Protestant church, my attendance in any church or synagogue has for many years been limited to formal occasions such as funerals, weddings, and Bar or Bat Mitzvahs.

But the reception I received as the brother of treasured members was warm and embracing, something we humanists find difficult to duplicate.

Why? Well, because we simply don't have such meeting places which weekly spew out the set, monotheistic rituals of subservience combined with their endless assurances of love and survival.

Full stop. And don't forget, as E.O. Wilson reminded us, we are all members of a tribe or more than one and in gaining tribal membership in these churches for many involves the enhancement of commercial opportunity! Yes, I buy your religion, you buy my merchandise!!

As for the opportunity to use the bully pulpits of all religions to tout political positions, examples are so rife as to hardly bear repeating, but of course they do so daily in overwhelming flows, completely ignoring the laws which give them tax exemption in the USA and license elsewhere to run things.

The USA may not be quite an Ayatollah run Iran, but we surely are a Protestant, Catholic, Jewish, Moslem, Buddhist, you name it impacted nation. Hiding behind the free speech amendment of our Constitution presents for observance of separation a permanent conundrum to us all.

And it is not going to change as this article in Illinois Review describes:

> "According to Liberty Counsel, the Internal Revenue Service (IRS) has officially reported that it is not auditing churches because it does not have the

authority to take away churches' tax-free status.

For years, leftist groups, such as Americans United for the Separation of Church and State (AU), have used deception and fear tactics to censor the church and muzzle pastors. A recent letter to religious leaders by Executive Director Barry Lynn inaccurately said, "If the IRS determines that your house of worship has engaged in unlawful intervention, it can revoke the institution's tax-exempt status."

An IRS spokesman said last week that the agency has been inundated with complaints, but they are not going to do any audits because they do not have the authority to do so. "Churches are tax-exempt inherently," said Mat Staver. "They don't need a letter from the IRS to be tax exempt, so their tax-exempt status cannot be taken away by the IRS."

No church has ever lost its tax-exempt status for opposing or supporting a candidate for political office. Churches and pastors may speak on Biblical and moral issues. They can educate about the candidates' viewpoints. They can encourage people to vote and can assist them in getting to the polls. This year

Liberty Counsel has sent over 100,000 copies of its <u>Take Back America: Silence is NOT an Option</u> to pastors and church leaders around America, to encourage pastors and church leaders to speak truth to this generation.

More pastors have been involved this year than ever before, even pastors who have been silenced in the past. Rev. Billy Graham is running full-page <u>advertisements</u> in a number of newspapers across the country, urging voters to vote for candidates that support Biblical values of life, natural marriage, and religious liberty. "This is unprecedented for the world's best-known evangelist," said Staver. "Billy Graham has always steered clear of politics. In reality, Billy Graham has merely raised his prophetic voice like any preacher should when Biblical and moral values are placed in jeopardy by politicians," said Staver.

John MacArthur, a well-known pastor and author, who was against Christian political activism, has had a dramatic change of heart. "I was amazed that one of the historic parties in the U.S. adopted the sins of Romans 1 as their platform," said MacArthur in a recent Sunday morning <u>sermon</u>. "This is a new day in our country. Parties that used to differ on economics, now differ dramatically on issues that invade the realm of God's law and morality."

"I am beginning to see more and more pastors waking up and realizing that Biblical and moral issues are under attack, and they have no choice but to speak," Staver said. "This isn't politics; it is Biblical and moral issues that have been politicized."

Liberty Counsel is an international nonprofit, litigation, education, and policy organization dedicated to advancing religious freedom, the sanctity of life, and the family since 1989, by providing pro bono assistance and representation on these and related topics."

In fact, churches or religious places of worship need not apply as they are automatically exempt from taxes unless they have activities which engage in businesses which produce profits.

That will be very tough to determine in most cases <u>as this IRS quote demonstrates</u>:

"Congress has imposed special limitations, found in <u>section 7611 of the Internal</u>

Revenue Code, on how and when the IRS may conduct civil tax inquiries and examinations of churches. The IRS may begin a *church tax inquiry* only if an appropriate high-level Treasury official <u>reasonably believes</u>, on the basis of facts and circumstances recorded in writing, that an organization claiming to be a church or convention or association of churches may not qualify for exemption, may be carrying on an unrelated trade or business (within the meaning of IRC § 513), may otherwise be engaged in taxable activities or may have entered into an IRC § 4958 excess benefit transaction with a disqualified person."

That will indeed be the day, Folks. Then <u>there is this clear analysis</u> of why religions has a virtually law free, tax free, speech free, conduct free chance to attack those of us who will not kneel to the subservience of the beliefs of their fantasy land ideas.

"Every time I talk about <u>Pulpit Freedom Sunday</u>, I inevitably get a comment from an audience member that goes something like this, "You know, if churches just unincorporated, they wouldn't be subject to the IRS," or "Because churches aren't required to apply for tax exemption, they aren't subject to 501(c)(3) of the tax code."

People have told me that churches have willingly gagged themselves in exchange for tax exemption and that they should just unincorporate or give up their exemption letter from the IRS and they could then be free to do what they want. Behind these questions and statements lies an admirable heart for the independence of the church. But these also demonstrate a fundamental and potentially dangerous misunderstanding of the law.

This misunderstanding has been propagated in different ways through the years in movements, booklets, and websites. The basic argument is that churches are free and if they don't incorporate or ask for tax exemption from the government, then the IRS can't regulate them or force them to pay income taxes (or do anything else for that matter).

This view is wrong under the law as it exists today. But in order to understand this, we need to take a few steps back. Churches are unique in that they enjoy a special status under the tax code. Normally, to be considered exempt from income taxes, an organization must apply for an exemption from the

IRS and demonstrate that it meets the requirements to be considered one of the exempt categories of section 501(c) of the tax code. Every organization that does not fall within one of the exempt categories of section 501(c) of the tax code is considered taxable.

But churches are different. Under section 508(c)(1)(A) of the tax code, churches are exempt from applying to the IRS for tax exempt status. Thus, churches are automatically exempt from income taxes under the federal tax code without first applying to the IRS for recognition of exempt status."

Those of us who are members of so-called nonprofit organizations which advocate policy changes and are subject to very different rules about how we operate. Thus, the supreme irony!

These non-religious NGOs will forever be behind the capacity of the religious entities of the USA to advocate legislation in our so-called republic which our Founders wanted free from religious entanglements.

None of us favor limitations on free speech, save perhaps yelling "Fire" in a crowded theater, but the Snowden affair and the harsh WikiLeaks corporal sentencing prompts the question of how far for example the Catholic Church can go in urging its supplicants to ignore the Rule of Law and welcome all immigrants to American to fill the pews of its churches. Their Bishops are preaching that the only criteria is "Love them"!!, regardless of whether these aliens are legal or illegal, criminal or not, needed or unneeded, rich or poor, skilled or unskilled, young or old.

Makes one wonder if our beset government can ever govern sensibly in the face of these untrammeled religious forces.

CHAPTER 20

FINALLY THE CORRECT WORDS TO ARTICULATE OUR FATAL POPULATION GROWTH DILEMMA

25 January 2013

Describing mankind as a "plague on the Earth", veteran nature broadcaster Sir David Attenborough says we need to limit population growth or famines will do it for us.

Not that this individual is the first to spell out the major culprit of our increasing planetary woes. Certainly, Paul Ehrlich's prognostications and those of many others come to mind.

But here is the right LANGUAGE which should send shivers down the spines of all of us, not just the enlightened cognoscenti who have so ably put forth the facts on global warming, environmental degradation, and the likely collapse of civil society.

Who is this savant? Wikipedia tells us

> "Sir David Frederick Attenborough, OM, CH, CVO, CBE, FRS, FZS, FSA (born 8 May 1926) is a British broadcaster and naturalist.

His career as the face and voice of natural history programmes has endured for 60 years. He is best known for writing and presenting the nine Life series, in conjunction with the BBC Natural History Unit, which collectively form a comprehensive by survey of all life on the planet. He is also a former senior manager at the BBC, having served as controller of BBC Two and director of programming for BBC Television in the 1960s and 1970s. He is the only person to have won a BAFTA in black and white, colour, HD and 3D.

Attenborough is widely considered a national treasure in Britain, although he himself does not like the term. In 2002 he was named among the 100 Greatest Britons following a UK-wide vote. He is a younger brother of director, producer and actor Richard Attenborough."

Again, our colleague, Joe Bish, of Population Media has highlighted this signal announcement with these words and with these attached reference materials which we suggest you read and watch in full.

"You may have seen headlines in the past few days relating to Sir David Attenborough's recent remarks, which reportedly went something like:

"We are a plague on the Earth. It's coming home to roost over the next 50 years or so. It's not just climate change; it's sheer space, places to grow food for this enormous horde. Either we limit our population growth, or the natural world will do it for us, and the natural world is doing it for us right now."

Coverage has been robust!

Two items below relate to this story. First is a link to an article where you can hear a 5-minute MP3 audio report, in which Population Matters Chief Executive, Simon Ross, gives commentary on the Attenborough story.

Also providing commentary on the audio is Rob Bailey, a senior energy, environment and resources research fellow at the Chatham House think tank. Mr. Baily's concludes that: "We are now in a period where the earth's environment, climate, biodiversity and water resources are changing with unprecedented rapidity.... That is all the result of man's activities on the planet and it's going to have profound implications for us. So, I think there's a lot of truth in that statement, unfortunately."

Sir David Attenborough recommends population control to avoid "plague on the Earth"

See: http://english.ruvr.ru/2013_01_23/Sir-David-Attenborough-recommends-population-control/

Secondly is a story published at Live Science.

Filmmaker Sir David Attenborough Calls Humans a Plague

22 January 2013

Sir David Attenborough, the famed British naturalist and television presenter, has some harsh words for humanity.

"We are a plague on the Earth," Attenborough told the Radio Times, as reported by the Telegraph. "It's coming home to roost over the next 50 years or so."

Attenborough went on to say that both climate change and "sheer space" were looming problems for humanity.

"Either we limit our population growth, or the natural world will do it for us, and the natural world is doing it for us right now," he said.

Sir David is not the only naturalist who has warned of population growth outstripping resources. Paul Ehrlich, the president of the Center for Conservation Biology at Stanford University and author of "The Population Bomb" (Sierra Club-Ballantine, 1968) has long used language similar to Attenborough's. And in 2011, an analysis of species loss suggested that humans are beginning to cause a mass extinction on the order of the one that killed the dinosaurs.

When asked about Attenborough's comments on humanity as its own scourge, Ehrlich told LiveScience he "completely agree[d], as does every other scientist who understands the situation."

Even so, that doesn't mean forceful measures must be taken. "Government propaganda, taxes, giving every sexually active human being access to modern contraception and backup abortion, and, especially, giving women absolutely equal rights and opportunities with men might very well get the global population shrinkage required if a collapse is to be avoided," Ehrlich said.

In fact, providing free, reliable birth control to women could prevent between 41 percent and 71 percent of abortions in the United States, according to a study detailed in the Oct. 4, 2012, issue of the journal Obstetrics and Gynecology.

Other scientists also agreed to some extent with the heart of Attenborough's message.

"It's clear that increasing population growth makes some of our biggest environmental challenges harder to solve, not easier," said from Jerry Karnas, population campaign director for the Center for Biological Diversity in Tucson, Ariz.

Karnas added, however, "What's needed is not population control but a real emphasis on reproductive rights, women's empowerment, universal access to birth control and education, so more freedom for folks to make better, more informed family planning choices."

And population numbers would matter less for the planet's health if clean renewable energy were widely adopted as well as planning laws, he told LiveScience during an interview.

> Attenborough is famous for his "Life on Earth" series of wildlife documentaries, among other nature programming. In 2009, he became a patron of the Population Matters, a group that advocates voluntary population limitation. At the time, he released a statement saying, "I've seen wildlife under mounting human pressure all over the world and it's not just from human economy or technology — behind every threat is the frightening explosion in human numbers."
>
> Earth's population reached 7 billion people on or around Oct. 31, 2011, according to United Nations estimates."

In trying to determine routes to survival, one could readily say as a recent TED speaker Alexandra Paul did that the planet could not survive with more than 2 billion humans. She suggested everyone think about a one child family. This of course will not happen, but even 2 billion will not be sustainable should people around the world try and possibly attain the living standards developed countries have enjoyed for decades.

The Plague is upon us. The prospect raised by credible experts about world population reaching 10 billion or more suggests that the gentler routes to a population stabilization or reduction will not be forthcoming. Yes, full contraceptive access could be a major help, but its fulfillment on a timely basis is unlikely.

Life, as I have enjoyed it, will not be the lot of my children or theirs and I deeply regret this fact. However, Sir David has at least articulated the unspeakable truth — or as Walt Kelly's cartoon possum so beautifully put it at a time years ago when the gentler solutions were possible, "We have met the enemy and he is us."

CHAPTER 21

AN IDEA TO HELP SAVE EARTH

To: World All Leaders in all Countries:

In the last 70 years, you have promoted the addition of more than 5 billion people to <u>our planet</u>. And <u>81 million again</u> in 2020 even while The United Nations predicts we'll have <u>11 billion humans on Earth by 2100</u>. Why would you do that?

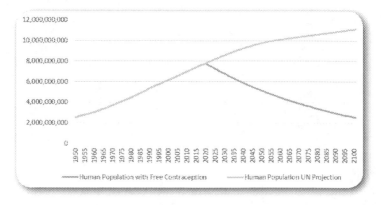

Believe it or not, renowned <u>scientists</u> told you we have decades to address Climate Change. Melting Himalayan glaciers creating lack of <u>fresh water</u> along with rising sea levels will spur poverty and epoch migration by 2040. As seen, technology begets broader and deeper consumption not less – <u>evidence plastics</u>.

A billion human use huge resources while two billion humans lack potable water and toilets. What if your goal was twofold, 1) as <u>E.O. Wilson</u> says, <u>leave fallow one half of Earth for nature</u> as an insurance policy for humanity's survival while protecting thousands of species from extinction and 2) raise all human quality of life to a U.S. quality of life where we live by 2100?

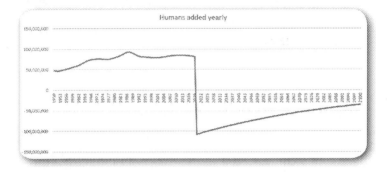

To do this, all we must do is eliminated <u>121 million unintended pregnancies every year</u> (and resultant abortions) returning human population back to our 1950 level of roughly 2.5 billion as <u>Sarah G. Epstein says, by giving free birth control to be used voluntarily by women and men of the world, empowering them to raise their living standards</u> where they live. We can do it if we want.

According to the U.S. Central Intelligence Agency (CIA) <u>more than half (130) of the (227) countries of the world have already achieved a total fertility rate (TFR) of less than replacement (2.1)</u>. Why can't the rest achieve this quickly? Even though the U.S. has a TFR of 1.84, Guttmacher Institute reports there are <u>millions of unintended pregnancies yearly resulting in more than a</u>

million abortions. Think about the pain and suffering and increased poverty this causes women and families.

Some families may volunteer to have two children or less to give all nature (grandchildren of the world) a chance for a good life. We urge you to educate and make contraceptives freely available to all women and men in the world regardless of their religion or geography right away at a cost of $20 billion per year Lester Brown reported in 2009 in his book *Plan B* on page 263.

A safe, effective, non-coercive, cost effective way to help now is for U.S. leaders to expedite FDA approval to replace surgical tubal ligation with nonsurgical QS chosen by 200,000 women in 50 countries as their method of permanent female contraception with no reported deaths or serious side effects. World leaders (and everyone) please act now!

ABOUT THE AUTHOR

Former U.S. Navy officer, banker and venture capitalist, Donald A. Collins, a freelance writer living in Washington, DC., has spent over 40 years working for women's reproductive health as a board member and/ or officer of numerous family planning organizations including Planned Parenthood Federation of America, Guttmacher Institute, Family Health International and Ipas. Yale undergraduate, NYU MBA.

OTHER BOOKS BY THE AUTHOR

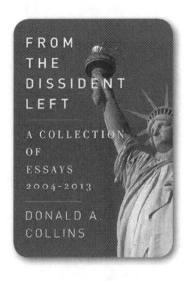

From the Dissident Left: A Collection of Essays 2004-2013
By Donald A. Collins
Publisher: Church and State Press (July 30, 2014)
ASIN: B00MA40TVE
Kindle Store

Trump Becoming Macbeth
By Donald A. Collins

Printed in the United States
by Baker & Taylor Publisher Services